W9-BMB-590

The Internet
for beginners

Philippa Wingate

Design, DTP and Illustrations by Andy Griffin

Technical consultant: Nick Bell
Additional consultancy by Thomas Barry
and Michael Sullivan
Edited by Jane Chisholm
Managing Designer: Mary Cartwright

SCHOLASTIC INC.
New York Toronto London Auckland Sydney

About this book

The Internet, also known as "the Net", can seem like a huge and confusing place. Every day you'll hear people talking about it, using jargon, buzzwords and technobabble.

Don't panic. As new software is developed and better techniques for exploring the Internet are introduced, it's becoming an easier place to find your way around. This book will make it even easier.

Net knowledge

The Internet for Beginners introduces you to the Net. It tells you what it is, how it works and describes all the fun and interesting things you can find on it.

The book includes a section telling you how to go "on-line" yourself, which means get connected to the Net. It details what equipment and software you need, and how to find a company which will give you access to the Net.

The Internet for Beginners introduces the main facilities the Net offers, and shows you how to use the programs that help you to explore them.

Getting help

On pages 38 and 39, there's a section covering some of the problems you may come across when using the Net. It explains what may be causing them and how to deal with them.

There are lots of new words connected with the Net. To help you, there's a glossary for quick reference on pages 43 to 45. Use the index on page 47 to find out where you can read fuller explanations of unfamiliar words. There's even a list of Internet slang on page 46.

Hot tips

You'll find a list of some of the companies that will give you access to the Net on page 41. On page 42, there's a selection of some of the interesting things you will find on the Net.

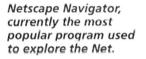

The Internet and its technology are changing rapidly. Information about it goes out of date quickly. Some things on the Net change or disappear, so it's difficult to guarantee that all the references in this book will remain correct. There is, however, lots of basic information that will be invaluable to a new user.

Netscape Navigator

There are many different Internet software packages available. At the time of writing, Netscape Navigator 2.01 was the most popular program for exploring the Net. It is used for most of the examples in this book.

If you have a computer already set up to use the Internet, you may have different software installed or you may have a different version of Netscape. Don't worry. Internet programs are often very similar. Using the examples in this book as a guide, you will be able to figure out how to use your own programs, even if some of their buttons and menu items have slightly different names.

Alternatively, on page 42, you can find out where to get your own copy of the Netscape Navigator program.

Netscape Navigator, currently the most popular program used to explore the Net.

What is the Internet?

The Internet is a vast computer network linking together millions of smaller networks all over the world.

On these pages you can find out exactly what a network is and how the computers on the Internet are connected to one another.

What is a network?

A network is the name given to a group of computers and computer equipment that have been joined together so they can share information and resources. The computers in an office, for example, are often networked so that they can use the same files and printers.

All the computers linked to the Internet can exchange information with each other. It's as easy to communicate with a computer on the other side of the world as with one that is right next door.

Once your own computer is connected to the Net it is like a spider in the middle of a huge web. All the threads of the web can bring you information from other computers.

Servers and clients

There are two main types of computers on the Internet. The ones which store, sort and distribute information are called hosts, or servers. Those that access and use this information, such as your computer at home, are called clients. A server computer serves a client computer, like a store owner helping a customer.

The picture below shows how the computer networks in different organizations in a town are linked together by the Net.

People can connect their computers at home to the Net.

At school, children can use the Net to learn and communicate with children in other countries.

Universities all over the world can use the Net to share their research information.

People can use the computers at this special café to access the Net.

Cables link one computer network to another.

Sometimes satellite links are used to link networks.

Telephone lines

The computer networks that make up the Net are linked together by private and public telephone systems. They can send and receive information along telephone lines. These lines range from cables made of twisted copper wires, to cables containing glass strands, that can carry lots of data at high speeds (over a thousand times faster than copper phone lines). Some networks can be linked by radio waves and microwaves. Networks in different countries and continents are often joined by undersea cables or by satellites.

Cables can run under seas and oceans.

The largest computers on the Net are connected by links known as backbones.

Connections

Some computers, especially ones used in large organizations such as universities, government departments and big businesses, have a "dedicated" Net connection. This means that they are linked to the Net all the time.

People using computers in homes and offices usually don't have dedicated connections. They can join or "hook up" to the Net by using the telephone to dial up a connection with a computer that is already on-line.

This computer belongs to a company that provides people at home or in offices with Net access.

Businesses can use the Net to sell their products.

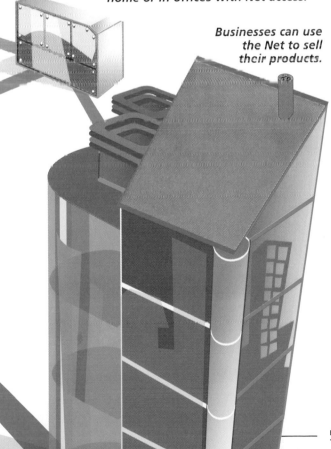

🌐 How big?

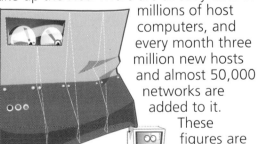

From huge supercomputers to small personal computers, all kinds of computers make up the Net. There are already tens of millions of host computers, and every month three million new hosts and almost 50,000 networks are added to it. These figures are increasing rapidly.

What's on the Net?

From games to gossip, messages to music, and shopping to academic research, once you have access to the Internet, you can do a huge variety of things. These pages show you just some of them.

Send messages.

Read a selection of cartoons.

Communicate by Internet telephone.

Information

There are many computers on the Net storing millions of files of information which are free for you to use. There are cartoons, art galleries, magazines and information which could help you with your work or hobbies.

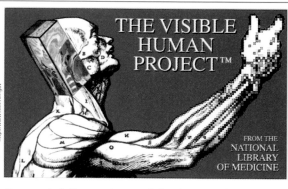

Research information and fascinating facts.

Listen to music or news on Internet radio.

Join in guided tours around museums and monuments.

Communication

There are millions of Net users all over the world with whom you can communicate, for work or for pleasure. You can send messages, chat, or take part in debates and discussions with other people who share your interests.

Look at beautiful pictures and photographs.

Services

Some computers on the Net provide you with services. You can use them to order flowers, get financial advice, find out train or airline times, book tickets for a show, check the weather report and catch some up-to-date news.

Play a wide selection of games.

Use a video telephone.

Find things just for kids.

Enjoy lots of great music and fan clubs.

Get a variety of financial information.

Check train timetables and ticket prices.

Look at up-to-date weather forecasts.

Programs

There are lots of programs available for you to copy onto your computer. Some are free to use; others you'll need to pay for. There are programs for playing games, listening to music or watching videos, as well as the latest programs to help you use the Net more efficiently.

Surfing in Cyberspace

Cyberspace is the name given to the imaginary space you travel in when you use the Net. Even though you stay in one place, you make an imaginary journey around the world by linking up to computers in different places. Moving around the Net is also known as "surfing".

How does the Net work?

Before two computers on the Internet can exchange information, they need to be able to find each other and communicate in a language that they can both understand.

Name and number

To enable computers on the Net to locate each other, they have unique addresses, called Internet Protocol (IP) addresses. IP addresses take the form of numbers. Numbers are difficult to remember, so each computer is also given a name, known as its domain name. The name has three main sections that give information about where the computer is located. Each section is separated by a dot.

Here's an imaginary domain name:

usborne.co.uk — *This name tells you what organization the user works in.*

usborne.**co**.uk — *This identifies the type of organization.*

usborne.co.**uk** — *This tells you the geographical location or country.*

Country codes

Many countries have their own code. Here are some you may come across:

au Australia
ca Canada
de Germany
fr France
nl Netherlands
se Sweden
uk United Kingdom

If an address has no country code, this usually indicates that a computer is in the USA.

Organizations

Here's a list of some of the codes for the types of organizations found in domain names:

ac an academic organization
co or **com** a commercial organization
edu an educational institution
gov a government body
net an organization involved in running the Net
org a non profit-making organization

Computer talk

To make sure that all the computers on the Net can communicate with each other, they all use the same language. It is called TCP/IP (Transmission Control Protocol/Internet Protocol).

TCP/IP ensures that when data is sent from one computer to another, it is transmitted in a particular way and that it arrives safely in the right place. If, for example, one computer sends a picture to another computer, the picture is broken down into small "packets" of data. Each packet includes information about where it has come from and where it is going to. The packets travel via the Net to the destination computer where they are reassembled.

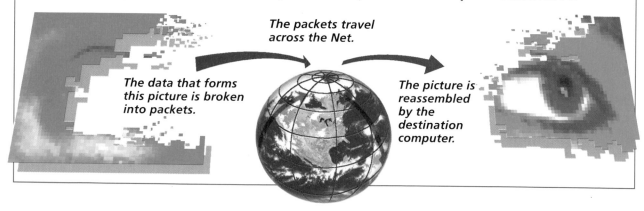

The packets travel across the Net.

The data that forms this picture is broken into packets.

The picture is reassembled by the destination computer.

Net history

Here's a brief history of how the Net began and how it became the worldwide network that it is today.

1960s The US Defense Department launched a project to design a computer network that could withstand nuclear attack. If part of the network was destroyed, information could be transmitted to its destination by alternative routes. The network became known as ARPANET (Advanced Research Projects Agency NETwork).

1970s Supercomputers in universities and companies throughout America were linked so that they could share research information.

1980s A new network called NSFNET (National Science Foundation NETwork) was set up.

This diagram shows the main connections on the NSFNET on a map of the USA.

NSFNET was a network exchanging non-commercial information.

1990s The network was opened up to everyone, including commercial companies and people using computers at home. The World Wide Web (see page 15) made the Net easier to use and, as a result, it expanded rapidly.

Who controls the Net?

Despite constant attempts by many governments and large organizations, nobody actually controls the Net. It is made up of lots of individual networks which are owned by somebody, but nobody owns all of it.

A test run on the Net

Now that you know the basics of what the Internet is and how it works, you should try it out.

You may find you belong to an organization that is already on-line. Many schools, colleges and universities have networks linked to the Net. Alternatively, you may work in an office that has computers on-line.

If you can't gain access in this way, ask a friend who is on-line to give you a demonstration.

You might find a local museum or library has Net access. Some bookstores and computer stores have computers on which you can explore the Net.

Another good way of trying out the Net is to go to a Cybercafé. These are special cafés where you can pay to use computers that are connected to the Net.

This Cybercafé is located in the Centre Georges Pompidou, in Paris.

Essential equipment

Whether you want to get connected to the Internet at school, at work or at home, you will need three essential pieces of equipment: a computer, a modem, and a telephone line. You will also need a selection of Internet software.

A computer

It is possible to connect to the Net with almost any computer. However, to make the most of all the facilities the Net offers, you will need at least a 486 DX33 IBM compatible PC, or a Macintosh 68030 series, or an Atari or Amiga computer of the equivalent power.

Your computer needs at least 4MB of RAM. RAM is part of your computer's memory. It is measured in bytes. A megabyte (MB) is just over a million bytes.

Special Net computers

Besides ordinary computers, there are two devices specifically designed for using the Net: network computers and set-top boxes.

Network computers are computers that can only be used to access the Net. They connect up to larger computers on the Net and use them to store and process data. They are different from ordinary computers, because they can operate with a smaller hard disk, which is the part of a computer where data is stored. They also need less memory, which is where data is processed. This makes network computers cheaper than normal computers.

A set-top box

Set-top boxes are devices that can be connected to a television. They allow you to access the Net, with your television's screen acting as a monitor. Set-top boxes are also cheaper to buy than ordinary computers.

A modem

To go on-line, you will need a modem. This is a device that enables computers to communicate with each other via telephone lines.

A modem converts the data produced by a computer into a form that can be sent along telephone lines. That data is received by a computer that is connected to the Net. It is then routed via the Net to its destination. The picture below shows two computers exchanging data.

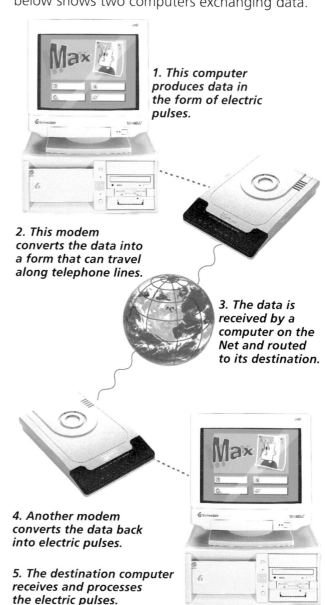

1. This computer produces data in the form of electric pulses.

2. This modem converts the data into a form that can travel along telephone lines.

3. The data is received by a computer on the Net and routed to its destination.

4. Another modem converts the data back into electric pulses.

5. The destination computer receives and processes the electric pulses.

Which modem?

You can buy three main types of modems: desktop modems, internal modems which fit inside your computer, and PCMCIA modems which are used with small, notebook computers.

Whichever modem you choose, make sure that it works with your kind of computer and that you have a telephone point near your computer that you can plug it into.

A PCMCIA modem is the size of a credit card.

Modem speed

When you buy a modem it is important to consider how fast it works. The speed at which modems transfer data to and from the Net is measured in bits per second (bps).

When using the Internet, it is a good idea to use a modem which operates at a speed of at least 28,800 bps. These modems are becoming increasingly cheap to buy.

When you dial up a connection to the Net, it's just like making an ordinary telephone call. A high speed modem reduces the amount of time you need to be on the phone, and that can save money.

Serial ports

An external modem plugs into your computer via a socket called a serial port. If you buy an external modem, you will need a high speed serial port to handle the speed at which data is being transferred.

Most modern computers will have high speed serial ports, but check your computer manual. If your computer doesn't have one, you can add one by buying a device called an expansion card.

Extras

Expansion cards are printed circuit boards which slot inside your computer to enable it to perform particular functions. For example, if you want to use the Net to listen to music, you'll need a sound card and speakers attached to your computer. If you want to watch video clips, consider buying a special graphics card to improve their appearance.

Expansion cards

Internet software

Most of the companies that provide you with a connection to the Net (see page 12) will supply all the software you need as part of their service. They will send you disks or a CD containing Internet software that is compatible with your computer and modem.

The software provided will usually include a dialer program to operate your modem and enable your computer to connect to the Net. There will be software that enables your computer to communicate with all the other computers on the Net. You should also be provided with a collection of programs that allows you to do things such as look at and copy files from the Net, send messages to other users, and join in discussion groups.

Once you are on-line, you can copy new Internet software onto your computer. Find out more about this on pages 32 and 33.

Providing access

Unless the computer you are using is permanently connected to the Net, you will need to pay a company to give you access. This company will act as your gateway to the Net by allowing you to hook up to their computers which are connected to the Net.

Two main types of companies offer this service: Internet service providers and on-line services.

Internet service providers

A company that provides access to the Net is called an Internet service provider (ISP) or an Internet access provider (IAP). There are many different companies available and more are appearing all the time. You will need to open an account with one. Some may offer you a free trial period of connection to the Net.

On-line services

An on-line service is a company that provides you with access to its own private network in addition to access to the Internet itself. The types of services offered on private networks range from international news to shopping facilities, business information, discussion groups, and a wide selection of entertainments.

Making choices

You'll find the phone numbers of a selection of Internet service providers and on-line services advertised in Internet magazines and local newspapers, with details of any special offers available. Each company offers different services, software and costs.

Phone up a company to make sure that they will provide the service best suited to your needs. Here are some of the key questions to ask:

Can I access your computer for the cost of a local call?
Large service providers have points of access to the Net all over the country. Each of these is called a node, or a

Point of Presence (POP).

Make sure that the service provider you choose has a POP near you, so that you only have to pay for a local telephone call to go on-line. This will be far cheaper than making a long distance call every time you use the Net.

What will my e-mail* address be?
Each Net user is given a unique address for sending and receiving e-mail. Some people like to use their name or nickname as part of their e-mail address.

Ask a service provider how much choice they can give you in choosing an address.

What costs can I expect?
Make sure that you understand exactly how much you will have to pay for your Internet connection. There is a list of the type of charges you can expect on page 13.

Try to avoid paying start-up costs, as you will lose this money if you decide to change service providers.

Find out whether there is a monthly fee and whether you will be charged for the amount of time you spend on-line.

If you are using an on-line service, check what fee you will have to pay for using their special services and their private network.

*You can find out about e-mail on page 27.

Costs

Different companies have different structures of costs for their services. Here are some of the costs you will come across:

Start-up cost - You may have to pay to open an account with a service provider.

Monthly fees and **time charges** - In some countries, such as Great Britain, local telephone calls are charged by the second. Most service providers in these countries do not charge for the amount of time a user spends on-line and only charge a small monthly fee for using their services. Many on-line services, however, do charge for time spent on-line.

In countries such as the USA and Australia, where local telephone calls cost a fixed amount or nothing, service providers usually charge for the amount of time a user spends on-line. This discourages people from staying on-line all day, preventing others from using the Net.

Software - Some service providers will send you a CD or a number of floppy disks containing all the Internet software you will need to get started. The cost of this is usually included in the start-up fee. Other companies may charge you a fee to copy software from the Net. Find out more about this on page 33.

Opening an account

Once you have decided to open an account, you'll need to give your service provider your name, address and telephone number.

Make sure that you tell them what kind of computer you are using so that they send you the correct Internet software.

What software do you supply?
Different companies supply different Internet software. If a friend has recommended a particular program, you may want to ask if it is available.

Do you provide access for the type and speed of modem I have?
Make sure that the modems (see page 10) used by a service provider can communicate efficiently with your modem.

The speed of the modems they use should not be slower than the speed of the modem connected to your computer.

Do you have enough modems so that I can connect at peak times?
Each person who dials up a service provider's computer needs a separate modem to make their connection. There are certain times of day when a lot of people use the Net. If all a service provider's modems are being used, you will get a busy signal and won't be able to get a Net connection.

Think about when you are most likely to use the Net and ask the service provider what its busiest periods are. Ask what its modem to customer ratio is.

Do you have a helpline?
Most service providers have a telephone helpline to give you advice on how to install and use your Internet software. Make sure that this helpline is available at the times when you are most likely to be using the Net, such as during the evening or at weekends.

Connecting and disconnecting

Once you have your equipment set up and your software installed, you are ready to connect up to the Internet for the first time. If your computer is not permanently connected to the Net, you will need to dial up a connection to your service provider's computer.

Dial up a connection

Open the window that contains a menu of the Internet facilities your service provider offers. This window may contain a button or menu item that instructs your modem to begin to dial up a connection. If not, select one of the Internet facilities, such as the World Wide Web, to start up your modem automatically.

This is part of the connection window of a service provider called Pipex Dial.

The Connect button

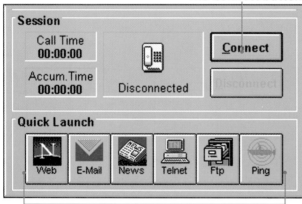

These buttons will start up your modem and take you straight to a particular Net facility.

Password

A box may appear asking you to supply a password. This password will be given to you by your service provider.

Your modem

Once your modem starts working, you may see flashing lights (if the modem is on your desktop) and hear dial tones. When it connects to the service provider's computer, you may hear strange squealing and fizzing sounds.

Connected

Once you are connected, an icon or message will tell you that your dial-up has been successful.

Your window may have a display that begins to time how long you have been connected to the Net.

No connection?

It may be more complicated than you think to get all the software correctly installed and your modem working. Don't hesitate to call your service provider's helpline with any problems. They should be able to help you.

When you are satisfied that your software and equipment are working, you may still be unable to get a connection. A message may appear saying your dial-up has been unsuccessful. Look at page 38 to find out why this may happen.

Warning

With some Internet connections you will automatically be given the choice of disconnecting after a certain period of time. This is a safeguard against spending hours on-line and possibly running up an enormous phone bill. If your software doesn't do this, be careful not to leave your computer connected to the Net for long periods.

Disconnecting

To disconnect from the Net, select the disconnect button or menu item.

The World Wide Web

The World Wide Web, also known as the Web or WWW, is probably the most exciting part of the Net. Art galleries, magazines, music samples, sports, games, educational material and movie previews are all available on the Web. It's not only interesting, but it's easy to use too.

Web pages and Web sites

The Web is made up of millions of documents called Web pages. These pages are stored on different computers all over the world. A collection of Web pages run by one person or organization is called a Web site. A computer containing one or more Web sites is called a host or server.

Browsers

To take a look at Web pages, you need a piece of software called a browser. If you have the Microsoft Windows 95, Macintosh System 7 or OS/2 Warp operating systems you will probably already have a browser. The software provided by a service provider should include a browser.

Starting your browser

To start your browser, connect up to the Net and select the Web button or menu item in your menu window. Your browser window will open. The Netscape Navigator browser window is shown below. Most browsers will have similar features.

When you launch your browser, a Web page may automatically appear in its window. This may be your browser's or service provider's "home page". A home page allows you to see what is available on the other pages that make up a Web site. It is like a contents page, or a store window which shows you what you can buy in the store. It is the page from which you start exploring a site. You will come across many home pages on the Web.

The Netscape Navigator browser window

The Home button - Click here to come back to your chosen home page.

The name of the browser

The menu bar contains your menu options.

The Location box contains the name of the page currently displayed.

This picture moves while the browser is searching for Web pages.

The window in which the pages are displayed. This is the home page for the company that produces Netscape.

This box displays information about what the browser is doing.

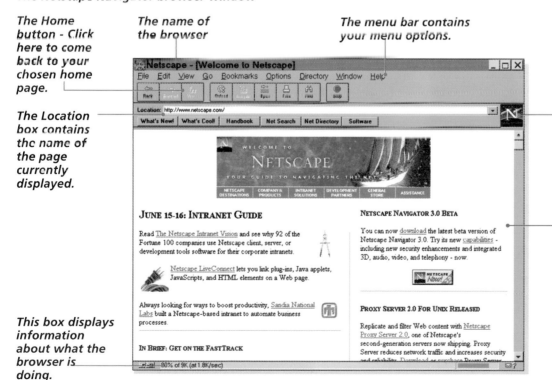

Web pages

The Web is made up of millions of pages of information. Despite its vast size, it's easy to find your way around, because every page has an address and all the pages are interlinked.

Web addresses

The addresses given to pieces of information on the Net, such as Web pages, are called URLs (Uniform Resource Locators). They may look complicated, but they are simple to understand.

The imaginary URL below shows the three main parts of an address:

> http://www.usborne.co.uk/public/homepage.htm

The first part, the "protocol name", specifies the type of document the page is. **http://** tells you that the page is a Web page. Some pieces of information have different protocol names, such as **ftp://** (see page 32).

> http://www.usborne.co.uk/public/homepage.htm

The second part, the "host name", is the name of the computer on which the page is stored.

> http://www.usborne.co.uk/public/homepage.htm

The final part, the "file path", specifies the file in which the page is stored and the name of the directory in which that file can be found.

The URL shown above tells you that the page is a Web page. It is stored on a site belonging to a company called Usborne in the UK. The file containing the page is called homepage.htm, which is found in a directory called public.

⚠ Be careful

When you write down or type a URL, make sure that you copy it exactly. There are no spaces between letters. Take note of where capitals are used and where lower case letters are used.

Finding a Web page

To find a particular Web page for which you have a URL, you need to be on-line. Type the URL into your browser's window and press the Return key. In Netscape Navigator you type the URL into a box named the Location box.

When a page appears in your browser window it is said to have been "downloaded". This means that its contents have been stored in your computer's temporary memory. Even if you disconnect from the Net, you'll still be able to see the page.

Give it a try

Try typing in the following Web address so that you can have a closer look at a Web page:

http://www.nasa.gov/

The home page of the National Aeronautics and Space Administation (NASA) in the USA will appear in your browser's window.

Type the URL in this box.

The Netscape logo moves while the browser is downloading a page.

This line shows you the size of an incoming page and how much of it has been downloaded.

Use the scroll bars to view the whole page.

Hypertext

Although pages on the Web may look like the pages in a book, if you look closely they have words and pictures that are underlined or highlighted. These are known as hypertext links. They are used to interconnect all the pages on the Web.

When you point to a hypertext link on a page, your pointer changes into a hand symbol like this.

If you click on the link, a new page containing related information will be downloaded. The link may take you to another page on the same site or to a site somewhere else on the Net.

When you point at a hypertext link, the URL of the page to which you will be transferred is displayed in your browser window.

The picture below shows how you can use hypertext to jump between pages.

This is a hypertext link. Click on this picture to go to a new page.

Welcome to the Gallery

Clicking on this hypertext picture will take you back to the home page.

Pages are interlinked like a vast spider's web.

This link will take you to an ultraviolet photograph of the Earth.

Clicking on the underlined words in this list will take you to a selection of photographs.

Browsing the Web

Moving from one page to another on the Web is called browsing, or surfing.

When you have browsed through several pages, you can use the Back and

Forward buttons to go back to previously viewed pages or forward again.

You can click the Home button at any time to return to the home page selected in your browser.

Exploring the Web

There are many interesting sites for you to visit on the Web, but you don't always know where to begin. This section shows you some of the techniques you can use to explore the Web.

Search services

A number of search services on the Web help you to find Web pages with information on specific subjects, without knowing their URLs. There are two main methods they use to search. Some use a key word search system, while others use a series of menus to find the subject you require.

Your browser may have a button or a menu item which brings up a list of the search services available. In Netscape Navigator, for **Net Search** example, the button is called *Net Search*.

Word search

To use a search service which searches by key word, type in a word or words which describe the subject you are searching for. The search service will then search through its index of millions of pages and present you with a list of pages that contain your word or words.

Say, for example, you wanted to find out about rockhopper penguins using the search service called AltaVista. Go to the AltaVista home page at the following URL:

http://altavista.digital.com/

On the home page is a search box. Type in the following: **+rockhopper** and **+penguin** and then click the *Submit* button to start the search.

A list of relevant pages will appear on

your screen. Choose one and click on its hypertext link to download the page into your browser.

Use your browser's Back button if you want to return to the list to select another Web page to look at.

AltaVista at work

Click on the hypertext links in the list to jump to new pages.

A list of penguin pages

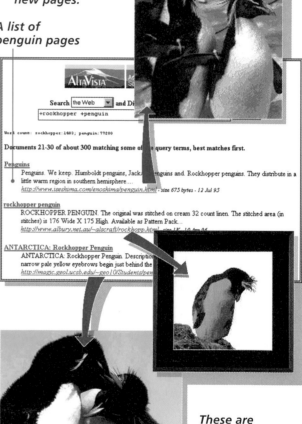

These are some of the pages you will find.

⚠ Be careful

Each search service has a slightly different system of entering key words. Make sure you follow the instructions a service gives. This will ensure that you find Web pages which cover the information you want.

Menu search

A menu-based search service divides the information on the Web into subject areas. It gives the user a series of subject menus to choose from, that gradually narrows down the subject area.

Yahooligans! is specially set up to find Web pages that will appeal to young people. It's part of a larger search service called Yahoo!. Go to its home page at:

http://www.yahooligans.com

If, for example, you want to use Yahooligans! to find a museum, click on Art Soup. From the next menu choose Museums and Galleries. When a list of options appears, click on the hypertext link of the item that particularly interests you.

Using menus to find a Web page

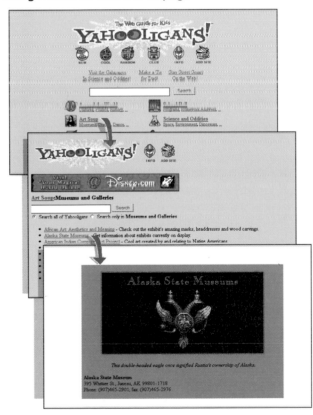

Cool sites

If you don't want to look at anything specific on the Web, you can just sample some of the great things out there in cyberspace. There are several useful places where you will find lists of new and interesting sites.

Browser buttons Your browser may have a button or menu item that will display a regularly updated list of new and interesting sites. This will contain hypertext links that will take you straight to the Web pages described. In Netscape Navigator, for example, there's a *What's Cool* button and a *What's New* button.

| What's New! | What's Cool! |

What's New Web pages With the Net expanding rapidly, hundreds of new sites come on-line every day. There are many Web pages devoted to listing what is new. Some of these are simply a collection of all the new pages, others only include the URLs of pages that the lists' compilers think are worth visiting.

Magazines and directories You will find a wide selection of Internet magazines and directories available that contain URLs and descriptions of new and exciting Web pages.

Newsgroups and mailing lists If you join on-line discussion groups called newsgroups (see page 22) and mailing lists (see page 31), you may be guided toward interesting pages by other members of the group. There are newsgroups, such as **comp.internet.net-happenings**, that are specially set up to discuss new sites.

These pages contain tips on how to become a really expert Web surfer. Find out how to find and download pages quickly. You can save text and pictures from Web pages onto your computer's hard disk.

If you have any problems downloading pages, find out some of the causes on page 38.

Speed surfing

Some Web pages take a long time to download, particularly if they include pictures. To speed things up, you can instruct your browser to download only the text on a page.

Your browser should have a menu item called *Auto Load Images*, or something similiar. (In Netscape Navigator this is in the *Options* menu.) When this item is selected, images will be downloaded automatically. Make sure this item is not selected. Now, when you download a Web page, small icons will appear in place of any pictures on the page. Be careful. Some pages look a little confusing if you don't download the pictures, and you may find it difficult to use their hypertext links.

This is the picture icon that appears in Netscape Navigator.

Stop!

You can stop a page downloading at any time by pressing the Stop button on your browser.

Bookmarks

As you explore the Web, you'll find pages that you want to look at regularly. Football fans, for example, might want to keep up with their team's latest results. Instead of trying to remember the URLs of these pages, you can add their names to a special list so that you can find them easily.

To add a page to this list, download it. In Netscape Navigator, open the menu called *Bookmarks*. Click on *Add Bookmark*. (With other browsers this facility may have a different name, such as Hotlist.) To download a marked page, all you have to do is open the Bookmarks window and double-click on its name in the list.

Netscape's Bookmarks window

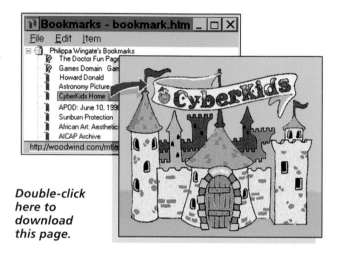

Double-click here to download this page.

Saving Web pages

Some pages disappear from the Web or are changed, so you may want to save certain pages onto your computer's hard disk.

To do this, download the page and select *Save As* in the *File* menu. In the Save As dialog box give your page a filename and specify where you want to save it. In the *Save file as type* section select *Source* and then select *OK*. This saves the page with its layout and hypertext (the pictures are not saved).

To look at your saved page you don't have to be on-line. Open your browser and select *Open File* in the *File* menu. Select the name of your file and click *OK*.

Save your page using a Save As dialog box.

Saving pictures

To save a picture on a Web page, click on it with your mouse (if you are using a PC, use your right mouse button). In the menu that appears, select the option to save the image. In the Save As dialog box that appears, choose a name and location for the picture and click *OK*.

These cartoons have been saved from an Internet football magazine.

Helper applications

As you surf around the Web, you may find files that your browser cannot handle. These pages often include video clips or sound clips. A message box may flash up on your screen telling you that you don't have the right software to view a page correctly. You will need to add "helper applications" to your browser to enable it to handle these files.

The message box usually includes advice about what software you need and how to download it. Follow the instructions provided.

Java Programs

Java is a computer programming language that enables Web pages to contain special features. These features include short animations, continually updated information and interactive features. (This means that you can take part in what happens, and choose the things you want to see or hear by clicking on screen.)

You will need to download a Java helper application to see these special features.

A Java program makes the planets on this Web page whizz around.

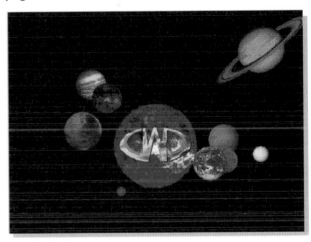

To find out more about Java, you can visit the Java home page at **http://java.sun.com/**.

Publishing your own Web pages

Once you become familiar with using the Web, you may find that you want to create your own Web pages. You'll need to find someone who will allow you to store your pages on their computer. Many service providers supply a small amount of space on their computers free with your Internet connection. Alternatively, you can hire space for a small monthly fee.

There are many software packages available which will help you design and construct your own Web pages.

Newsgroups

By joining discussion groups called newsgroups, you can use the Net to get in touch with people who share the same interests as you. Most newsgroups discuss very little actual news – a lot of it is chat and trivia, but it's fun!

Usenet newsgroups

Newsgroups form a part of the Net called Usenet. There are over 15,000 newsgroups available for you to join. Each one has a single theme, covering interests and hobbies, from jazz music to jets, from jokes to jobs.

Some newsgroups are dedicated to discussion, while others are more like helplines where you can ask questions and get advice from the experts around the world.

When you join a newsgroup, a copy of all the articles recently written by members of the group will be sent to you. You can read these articles, write your own, or join in ongoing debates.

Newsgroup names

Each Usenet newsgroup has a unique name. The name acts as a guide to its theme. The name has two main parts. The first part describes what basic topic the group covers, such as science or computing.

The following are the abbreviations used for some of the main newsgroup topics:-

alt.   Alternative newsgroups. These cover all kinds of topics, but usually in a humorous, crazy and alternative way.

biz.   Business newsgroups. These cover discussions of new products, ideas and job opportunities.

comp.   Computing newsgroups. These cover everything to do with computing and

computer technology. They are great places to start looking for expert help.

misc.   Miscellaneous newsgroups. These cover subjects such as health, kids, and books which don't fit any other topic group.

news.   Newsgroup newsgroups. These offer tips and advice for people using Usenet for the first time.

rec.   Recreational activities newsgroups. These cover sports, hobbies and games, from skateboarding to sewing.

sci.   Scientific newsgroups. These are mainly used by academics to discuss their research.

soc. and **talk.**   Social and talk newsgroups. These offer the opportunity to discuss and debate social issues, different cultures, politics, religion and philosophy.

The second part of a newsgroup name, known as its subtopics, narrows down the topic area the group concerns. For example, an imaginary newsgroup name might be **rec.music.presley**. This tells you that the newsgroup is in the recreational activities topic group. Its subtopic is music, more specifically the music of Elvis Presley.

Newsgroup access

Most service providers will give you access to Usenet newsgroups as part of your Internet package. They should supply you with a program called a newsreader, which enables you to read and send newsgroup articles.

Some browsers, such as Netscape Navigator, include a newsreader facility. For this, you will need to open a special newsreader window.

Opening your newsreader

Once you are on-line, open your newsreader window. First you need to display a list of the names of all the newsgroups available. To do this, select the button or menu item which invites you to view all newsgroups. In the Netscape News window, you should select *Show All Newsgroups* in the *Options* menu. A list like the one below will appear.

You need to be on-line so that you can look at this list. Your computer will download it from a computer called a news server. Once it has been downloaded, you can disconnect while you look at it.

Choosing a newsgroup

Scroll through the list of newsgroup topics, opening topic folders to see which subtopics they contain. If, for example, you wanted to find a group that discussed mountain biking, you would click on **rec.*** to see a list of its subtopics. Next you would click on **rec.bicycles** and, finally, on **rec.bicycles.offroad**.

Subscribing

To subscribe to a newsgroup, simply locate its name in the list and select a subscribe button or menu item. In the Netscape News window you click in the box beside the group's name. You don't have to pay to join a Usenet newsgroup.

Unsubscribing

To unsubscribe from a newsgroup, click in the box so that the check mark disappears, or select an unsubscribe button or menu item.

A list of newsgroups in a section of the Netscape News window

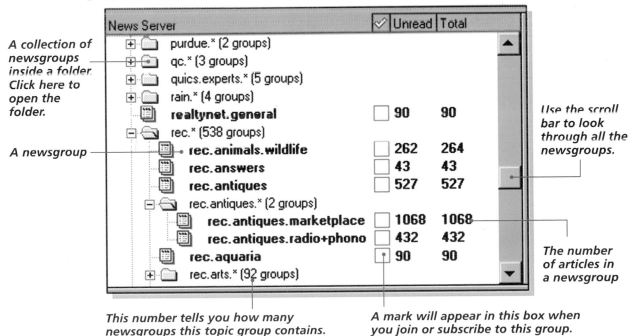

A collection of newsgroups inside a folder. Click here to open the folder.

A newsgroup

Use the scroll bar to look through all the newsgroups.

The number of articles in a newsgroup

This number tells you how many newsgroups this topic group contains.

A mark will appear in this box when you join or subscribe to this group.

Posting to newsgroups

As a new member of a newsgroup, you'll be known as a newbie. It's fun to get involved in debates and discussions or ask for information and advice. On these pages you'll find out how to join in by receiving and sending newsgroup articles.

Collecting articles

Messages sent to newsgroups are called articles or postings. Once you have subscribed to a newsgroup, a computer called a news server will send you a copy of all the articles that have recently been posted to that group.

To collect these articles, you need to be on-line. Open your newsreader window. A number will appear beside the name of each of the newsgroups you belong to. This number indicates how many new articles are currently available in the newsgroup.

Reading articles

Click on the name of the newsgroup that you want to look at. A list of all the new articles in it will appear. Click on the name of an article to download it.

You should disconnect from the Net before you read articles, because you don't want to pay for a long telephone connection.

Keeping track

Once you have read an article, your newsreader will mark it as "read". This means that the next time you come back to the newsgroup you won't see that message. This ensures that only new articles you haven't read before are displayed in the list.

Check regularly to see if you have received anything from your newsgroup, because most news servers delete articles after a few days.

This is the Netscape News window showing an article open.

Number of articles currently in each newsgroup

A list of the newsgroups to which the user is subscribed

Click here to see the articles in this newsgroup.

A list of articles in the alt.cybercafes newsgroup

Click to open an article.

This article has already been read.

The text of an article

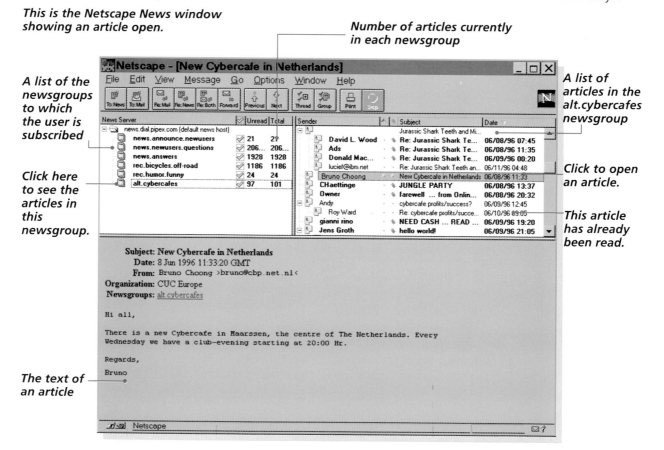

Lurking

When you first join a newsgroup, don't start posting articles right away. Spend a couple of days reading the ones written by other members first, to get an idea of what kind of discussions are currently in progress. This is called lurking.

Frequently Asked Questions

Most newsgroups have a Frequently Asked Question (FAQ) article. This is a list of the questions most often asked by new members. It saves other members from having to answer the same questions again and again. The FAQ article will appear every couple of weeks. Read it before you start posting.

Ready to post

When you post an article to a newsgroup, you have three options: you can start a new discussion, join in an existing one, or e-mail (see page 27) a personal response to someone else's article. Starting a new discussion is known as starting a new thread. To do this, open your newsreader window. Click on the name of the newsgroup to which you want to send your article. Click the *To: News* button. A message composition window will appear.

Compose your article in a message window.

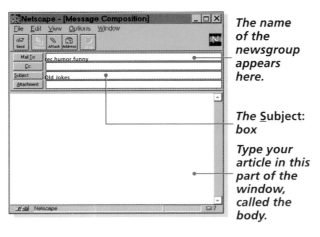

The name of the newsgroup appears here.

The Subject: *box*

Type your article in this part of the window, called the body.

Summarize the contents of your article in the *Subject:* box, so that people scanning through the list of articles will know if your article will interest them. Write your article in the area of the composition window called the body. For some advice on writing articles, see page 26.

When your article is ready, connect to the Net and select the send button or menu item.

Responding

There are two ways in which you can respond to an existing article. The first is by sending a reply to the newsgroup. This is known as following up. The second is by responding personally to the author of an article by sending them an e-mail. This is called replying.

Open the article you want to respond to. To follow up, select *Re:News*. To reply personally by

e-mail select *Re:Mail*. (It is considered good manners to send an e-mail to the author of an article you are following up. To do this, press *Re:Both*.)

A window will appear in which you can type your message. The *Mail To:* box will automatically be addressed and the body of the message will contain a copy of the article to which you are responding. Edit it down to the points your article is answering.

Compose your message, connect to the Net, and then select the send button or menu item.

✉ **Tips**

You can join a newsgroup called **news.announce.newusers** for advice on using Usenet newsgroups.

If you want to check that you are posting articles correctly, you can send a message to **misc.test**. You will automatically get a reply to your message a few days later.

Netiquette

There aren't many rules about what you can and can't do on the Net, but there are things that are considered good and bad manners. Users have developed a code of conduct known as Netiquette. Here are some rules to follow when composing articles for newsgroups or sending e-mail (see opposite).

Keep it brief

Make sure everything you write is brief and to the point. Express yourself as clearly and concisely as you can. People have to download your articles, and the longer they are, the more time and money they will cost to download.

Watch your tone

When you are talking with someone on the telephone, it's easy to know whether they are being funny or sarcastic by the tone of their voice. When typing a message, however, it's hard to show emotion. Some Net users put words in brackets to indicate their state of mind, such as <grin> or <sob>.

Another way of showing emotion on the Net is to use little pictures called smileys or emoticons. They are made up of keyboard characters and when you look at them sideways they are like faces. New smileys are being made up all the time. Here are some useful ones.

:-D	Laughing	:-P	Tongue out
:-(	Sad/angry	:-/	Confused
:-)	Happy/sarcastic	:*	Kissing
:-X	Not saying a word	0:-)	Angel
:-O	Wow!	$-)	Greedy
:*)	Clowning around	:-I	Grim
I-O	Bored	:`-)	Crying

Use an acronym

To avoid too much typing, some Net users have taken to using "acronyms", which are abbreviations of familiar phrases. They usually use the first letter of each word. Here are some of the most commonly used acronyms:

BTW	By The Way
DL	DownLoad
FYI	For Your Information
IMHO	In My Humble Opinion
OTT	Over The Top
POV	Point Of View
TIA	Thanks In Advance
TTFN	Ta Ta For Now
UL	UpLoad
WRT	With Reference To

No shouting and flaming

When you type a message, don't use UPPER CASE letters, because in Net speak this is the equivalent of shouting. It is considered rude and will annoy your fellow Net users. If you break the code of Netiquette or post an article that makes someone angry, you will get "flamed". This means that you will receive lots of angry messages, known as flame mail, from other users.

No spamming

Spamming is Internet slang for sending a huge number of useless or rude messages to a single person or site. The word is also used to describe a technique used by certain businesses which send messages advertising their products to thousands of different users via the Net.

E-mail

Electronic mail, known as e-mail, is a method of using your computer to send messages to other Net users. It's a great way of communicating. With e-mail you can send messages more quickly and cheaply than normal mail. An e-mail sent from London can arrive in Tokyo in under a minute and only cost the same as a local telephone call. Net users call the normal mail "snail mail" because it's so slow!

E-mail addresses

With e-mail, as with normal mail, you need to know someone's address before you can send them a message. Everyone on the Net has a unique e-mail address. When you start an account with a service provider you'll be given your own address.

An e-mail address has two main sections: the username and the domain name. The username is usually the name or nickname of the person using e-mail. (One on-line service called CompuServe uses a number instead of a name.)

The username is followed by an @ symbol, which means "at".

The domain name gives information about the computer and its location. (You can read more about domain names on page 8.)

Here's an imaginary e-mail address:

philippa@usborne.co.uk

Username	**Domain name**	**Country**
At		**Code**

@ Tip

Some e-mail addresses are fairly complicated, so make sure that you write them down *very* carefully.

How does e-mail work?

When you send an e-mail message from your computer, it is delivered to a computer called a mail server. From there, it is transferred across the Net, via a chain of mail servers, until it arrives at its destination.

E-mail software

The software package supplied by your Internet service provider should include a program which will enable you to send and receive e-mail.

Two of the most popular programs currently available are Eudora and Mail-It. If you are using Microsoft Windows 95 or Macintosh System 7, you will probably already have e-mail software installed on your computer.

An e-mail window

Open your e-mail program window. The example screen shown below is the Netscape Mail window. It shows some of the main parts of an e-mail window. Other e-mail program windows will share many of the same features.

The Netscape Mail window

These are the folders in which incoming and outgoing mail is stored.

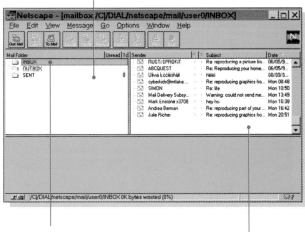

The INBOX folder is open.

This window shows what messages are currently stored in the INBOX folder.

Sending e-mail

On these pages you can discover exactly how to send an e-mail to another Net user anywhere in the world. Find out how to create a handy address book for the e-mail addresses of any friends to whom you want to send messages regularly.

Preparing an e-mail

Open your e-mail program window and select the button or menu item for composing a new message. A window will open. Netscape Mail's Message Composition window is shown below. It consists of a header section and a body section. Type your message into the blank body section. (You will find some advice on writing e-mail on page 26.)

Filling in a header

Before you can send an e-mail you have to fill in the header section. This is like writing the address on the front of an envelope to make sure the letter inside reaches its destination.

In the *Mail To:* box, type the e-mail address of the person to whom you are sending the message. Add the address of anyone you want to send a copy of your e-mail to in the *CC:* box.

Choose an informative subject line to fill in the *Subject:* box. Many Net users receive lots of e-mail, including junk e-mail which is mostly advertising. Use the subject line to give the person who receives your e-mail an idea of what is contained in your message. This ensures that he or she won't just delete the message without reading it. The subject lines appear in a list of messages stored on your computer. They act as a useful reminder of what each e-mail is about.

Netscape Mail's Message Composition window

The header section

Click here to send your e-mail.

The e-mail address of the recipient goes here.

The subject line

Netscape - [Message Composition]

File   Edit   View   Options   Window

Send   Quote   Attach   Address   Stop

Mail To: ▶ philippa@usborne.co.uk

Cc:

Subject: Good luck

Attachment:

Dear Philippa
It was great to see you.
Good luck with the play next week. I hope it goes well. Make sure you break a leg :-)
Let me know when you will be back in the summer and we will meet up again.
Take care.
John

The body section

@ Tip

If you are charged by the minute for the time you are on-line, write your e-mail before you connect up to the Net. You can then take your time to make sure you are happy with your message before you spend money sending it.

Signing off

Many e-mail programs allow you to create a personal "signature" which automatically appears at the end of your messages.

Your signature can only be made up of letters and symbols from the keyboard. Some people use them to draw complicated pictures, while others will include a funny quotation. You could include the snail mail address and telephone number of your school or company.

The signatures shown below are pretty long. Ideally, you should make your signature no more than four lines. People will have to spend time and money downloading your e-mail file, so a long signature might make you unpopular.

If you want your signature to be included with an e-mail, you have to instruct your computer to attach it.

This signature is a picture made out of keystrokes.

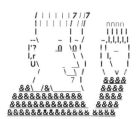

- * - * - * - * -
Jessica Hopf
Maxim School
35 Long Street
Townsville
tel 01876 4657
- * - * - * - * -

This signature includes a snail mail address.

Sending an e-mail

When you are ready to send an e-mail message, select the send button or menu item.

If you are connected to the Net already, your message should be sent right away. If you aren't connected, your computer will probably save the e-mail. Next time you dial up a Net connection, it will be sent.

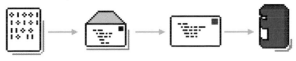

Your e-mail program may show an animation to tell you that your message has been sent.

An address book

Many e-mail programs let you create an address book containing the names and e-mail addresses of the people to whom you regularly send messages.

You can type e-mail addresses into your address book, or add addresses from e-mails you have already received.

To send a message to a friend, you usually only have to double-click on their name in your address book. A message composition window that is already addressed to them will open.

Netscape Mail's Address Book window

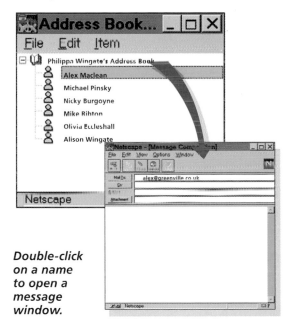

Double-click on a name to open a message window.

Finding an address

There isn't a directory listing the e-mail addresses of all the users on the Net. The easiest way to get someone's address is to call them and ask them. Get them to send you an e-mail to make sure that you don't write down the wrong address. Their address should appear at the top of their message.

Receiving e-mail

Any e-mail sent to you will be stored in a mailbox by your service provider. You can find out here how to collect, read and reply to it.

Reading an e-mail

To collect e-mail, you need to be on-line. Open your e-mail window and select the button or menu item that searches for new mail. Most programs have an icon or message that tells you when new mail arrives. Any mail will automatically be downloaded. You can then disconnect from the Net before you read it.

Many e-mail programs place new mail in a folder or in-box. When you open the folder, the messages will appear in a list detailing their sender, subject and date.

To read a message, double-click on its name in the list. It will appear, with a header section specifying its sender, subject and date, followed by the text of the message itself.

Replying to an e-mail

Many programs make it very easy to send a reply. You simply open the message you want to reply to and select a reply button or menu item. In Netscape Mail, this button is called *Re:Mail.* A message composition window will appear, with the *Mail To:* box addressed to the sender and the *Subject:* box filled in. The body of the message will contain a copy of the original e-mail. You can delete it or edit it down to remind the sender which message you are replying to.

Bouncing e-mail

Sometimes e-mail doesn't reach its destination. Any e-mail that fails to get through and is sent back to you is said to have "bounced". If your e-mail bounces right away, check that the address is correct. If it bounces after a couple of days, there has probably been an equipment failure on the Net. Try sending it again.

Send yourself e-mail

To try out your e-mail program, you can send an e-mail to yourself. Put your own e-mail address in the *Mail To:* box.

Alternatively, you can e-mail an organization called Mailbase. The address for the USA, Canada & South America is:

mail-server@rtfm.mit.edu

Leave the subject line blank and enter this message in the body:
send usenet/news.answers/internet-services/access-via-email.

Mailbase's address in Europe and Asia is:

MAILBASE@mailbase.ac.uk

Leave the subject line blank and enter this message: send lis-lis e-access-inet.txt

Attachments

Mailbase should send you back an e-mail including an "attachment" which contains more information about e-mails. An attachment is a file added to an e-mail. It can be a text, a picture or a sound file. To read an attachment you need to select a button or menu item in your e-mail window and follow the instructions you are given.

Mailing lists

A sure way of receiving lots of e-mail is to join one of the many mailing lists available via the Net. They are like newsgroups (see page 22), because you can discuss a wide variety of topics with other enthusiasts, but with mailing lists you send and receive articles by e-mail.

Finding a mailing list

To find an index of the mailing lists available on the Net, open your Web browser and type in the following URL:

http://www.Neosoft.com/internet/paml/bysubj.html

A menu of topic groups, like the one shown below, will appear. When you click on a topic in which you are interested, you will see a list of the mailing lists related to that topic. Click on the name of a list to see a brief description of the types of issues discussed by its subscribers.

A list of mailing lists available on the Net

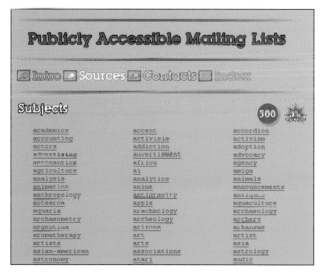

Subscribing to a list

The page containing a description of a mailing list should also include instructions about how to subscribe to it. Follow these instructions closely. Each mailing list has a slightly different system. It usually involves sending an e-mail to a specified address, with a specified subject line or message in the body of the e-mail.

Welcome

After you have subscribed to a mailing list, you should receive a reply to your e-mail within a few minutes or a few hours. Make sure you keep this "welcome" e-mail, as you may need to refer to it. The message will confirm you have joined successfully. It may also give you some rules of the list, the address to which you send e-mail and how to unsubscribe from the list when you want to.

Many mailing lists have administrators who oversee the messages sent in. In your welcome e-mail you may be told the e-mail address of the list administrator. You can e-mail them if you have any specific problems or questions.

What next?

As a member of a mailing list, you will receive a copy of all the e-mail sent to the list. Download these messages in the way you would download any e-mail (see page 30).

Sending e-mail to a list

To send a message to a mailing list, simply compose an e-mail message in the way described on pages 28 and 29. Send it to the address specified in your welcome e-mail.

Make sure you don't send any personal messages intended for the list administrator to the mailing list e-mail address by mistake.

Files via the Net

There are thousands of sites on the Net with files for you to copy onto your computer, from pictures to sound clips, from text files to Internet software. The main method of transferring files over the Net is called File Transfer Protocol (FTP), and the easiest way to use FTP is with a Web browser like Netscape.

Finding FTP files

FTP files are stored on computers all over the world, called FTP sites. They have addresses, called URLs (see page 16) which help you to find them. Their URLs begin with the letters **ftp://**.

When you are browsing the Web, you will probably come across Web pages which have hypertext links to FTP sites where you will find files to download. There's a long list of FTP sites at the following address: **http://hoohoo.ncsa.uiuc.edu/ftp-interface.html**

A good way to find FTP files is using a search service (see page 18) such as Infoseek, Yahoo!, or Lycos.

For example, you could use Infoseek to find a new browser program. Type the words **browser**, **software** and **best** into its word search box and click the Search Now button. In the list of URLs that appear, there might be some suitable FTP files. To download one of these FTP files, you would simply click on the hypertext link.

(Infoseek will charge you for its services, but it offers a free trial period.)

Permission

You often need permission or "authorized access" to download files from the Net, but there are lots of files that are available for anyone to use. These are called anonymous FTP sites, because you don't have to be a known user or use a special password before you copy files onto your own computer.

Using FTP

Whether you type the URL of an FTP site into your browser, or click on a hypertext link to an FTP site, your browser will automatically connect or "log in" to the computer where the files are stored.

Sometimes a file will automatically start downloading onto your computer. Alternatively, you may see a list of all the files available on the FTP site. Find the file you require and then click on it.

Downloading

Before your computer starts downloading a file, a *Save As...* dialog box will appear. You must give the file a name and select where you want to store it. Choose whether you want to save it on the hard disk of your computer or on a floppy disk. Finally, click the *OK* button.

A Save As... dialog box

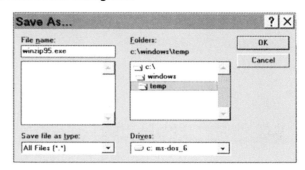

The file will start downloading. A *Saving Location* window will appear giving details about the file you are downloading and telling you how much of it has been downloaded.

A Saving Location box

This shows you how much of the file has already been downloaded.

Zipped up

Many FTP files are compressed or "zipped". This means they have been made smaller, so that they take up less room when stored on a computer's hard disk and can be transferred across the Net more quickly. A file or files compressed in this way is known as an archive.

Once a compressed file is copied onto your computer, you have to "decompress it", restoring it to its original size so that your computer can use it properly. It's a little like a beach ball; you let all the air out of it so that it fits in your bag to take to the beach. But once you are there, you blow the air back into it so you can use it.

Some FTP files will decompress automatically. If they don't, you will need a special program to decompress them. You can download one from the Net. Find out where to find one on page 42.

Internet software

Much of the latest Internet software is available to be downloaded from the Net. Some of these programs may be better or more up-to-date than the software supplied by your service provider. You may choose to download a new browser, such as Netscape Navigator, an e-mail program or a more recent version of a program you are already using.

On page 42 you'll find the addresses of some good software to download.

Is the software really free?

You will have to pay for some of the software you come across on the Net before you can download it. It is usually the same amount of money as if you bought the software package in a store.

There are many programs which you can download by FTP that are either free or available at a very small cost. They fall into three main categories: freeware, shareware and beta programs.

Freeware This is software that is completely free for anyone to copy onto their computer and use. The person who created the software has donated it free of charge.

Shareware This is software that you can install on your computer, but there are certain conditions attached. The most common condition is that you try out the program for an initial free trial period. If you like it, you then pay the person who owns it. The amount you pay is usually small.

When you have made your payment, the software company usually sends you the manual, notifies you if the software is updated and helps you if you have any problems using it.

Beta programs Beta programs are new programs that have been tested by the company that created them and are available for further testing by users. They may have mistakes and problems in them. If you find a fault (known as a "bug") in the program, you should inform the company who created it. Some beta programs are free; others will be charged for.

Cyberchat

E-mail and newsgroups are great ways of using the Net to make friends and communicate, but you do have to wait for a reply. Sometimes it's only a couple of minutes, but it can be a day or two. Today, there are facilities on the Net that allow you to communicate with other users instantly.

Internet phone

There are programs available that allow you to use your computer like a telephone. The Net can transmit sound in the same way that it transmits any other kind of data.

To talk to a friend on the Net, you will need a microphone, a pair of speakers connected to your computer, and a sound card (see page 11). The person you intend to talk to must have the same equipment. You will both need to download an Internet telephone program and you will have to pay for it.

Once you have installed your equipment and your program, you can dial up your friend's computer. When he or she answers, you can speak, just as on a normal telephone.

This is an Internet phone called WebPhone.

You can dial a telephone number by clicking on these buttons on screen.

One of the great advantages of using an Internet telephone is that you can call anywhere in the world for the price of the local call that connects your computer to your service provider's computer.

Video phones

Internet video phones allow you not only to talk to a person via their computer, but also to see them on your computer screen while you talk.

To use this system you will need a video digitizer and a video camera connected to your computer system. This will film you and transmit the data over the Net to another user. You will also need a microphone, speakers, sound and video cards, and a video phone program.

Conferencing

The Internet telephone and video phone systems described above have been further developed to allow several people to speak and watch each other at once. This enables people to have debates and discussions using the Net.

The quality of the sound and pictures achieved by these programs is getting better as the equipment and the speed of data transfer (see page 11) on the Net improves.

CU-SeeMe is a program used for video-conferencing.

✉ Finding software

You can find out where to go on the Net to download the software mentioned in this section in the list of sites and resources on page 42.

Internet Relay Chat

A popular Net facility is Internet Relay Chat (IRC). This allows you to have live conversations with other users, using your keyboard to type your conversations. As you type a message, it instantly appears on another user's screen. He or she can read it and type a reply.

The groups in which people meet to have chats are called channels. Some of them are dedicated to discussions about particular topics, such as football or computer games, while others are used for more general, sociable chat.

The IRC channels are controlled by special computers on the Net called IRC servers, which transmit all the chatting around the world.

IRC programs

To join in IRC, you will need a program called an IRC client program. This will interpret the data supplied by an IRC server. You can download an IRC client from the Net.

IRC is quite complicated to use. There are many codes and commands that you need to type in to tell your computer what you want it to do. So make sure that you read all the instructions that are downloaded with your IRC client program.

Virtual worlds

Another place to meet other Net users is in virtual worlds. These are imaginary 3-D worlds generated by computer. In a virtual world the scenery changes according to how you move. You can use your mouse or arrow keys to walk around. You can interact with things, such as picking up objects or opening doors.

One of the great things about virtual worlds on the Net, is that you will meet other users there. They appear on your screen as "avatars". An avatar is a body that represents a user and moves through a virtual world,

responding to instructions. An avatar may look like a bird, a cat, a goblin, or anything. You can talk to the other users you meet using your keyboard to type in your comments. Your words will appear on the screen for them to read.

An avatar

To enjoy virtual worlds you need special software, a powerful computer (at least a 486DX66 with 16MB of RAM), a fast modem (at least 28,800bps), and a video card.

Avatars in a virtual world called Worlds Chat

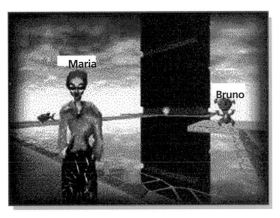

Maria

Bruno

Explore a virtual world called AlphaWorld.

Games on-line

If you like to play games on your computer or games console, there are lots of challenging games on the Net for you to download and play. But the best way of playing games is on-line.

Finding games

There are lots of places on the Net where you can find out about games. Many big games manufacturers, such as Sega and Nintendo, have their own home pages where you can read about their new products, get some hints and tips about how to play a particular game, and enter competitions.

Alternatively, you can use a search service (see page 18) to find information about a particular game you are interested in.

Here are some of the home pages you will find.

This site has links to video games.

Let's talk games

You can use the Net to get in touch with other games enthusiasts so that you can discuss tactics and expertise. There are many newsgroups and mailing lists dedicated to discussing individual games.

The best place to start looking for games newsgroups is in the **rec.games** folder in the list of newsgroups (see page 22). There are groups for the fans of games ranging from pinball to backgammon.

A screen shot from a 3-D computer game called **Grand Prix II**

Off-line games

From chess, to football, there are lots of games on the Net that you can download. Once a game is downloaded and stored in your computer's memory, you don't need to be on-line to play it.

On the Web page where a particular game is discussed, you will usually find a hypertext link that will take you to a site from which you can download the necessary software.

> ✉ **Useful addresses**
>
> On page 42 you will find a list of the URLs of many of the Web pages shown in this section. You will also find a selection of other great games sites.

On-line games

One of the great advantages of using the Net to play games is that you can play on-line against other users. For example, a user in Berlin can play on-line chess against a user in Tokyo. If you prefer fantasy games, you can take part in adventures with other users, fighting against them for prizes or teaming up with them to quest and battle together.

Watch an on-line chess game or take part yourself.

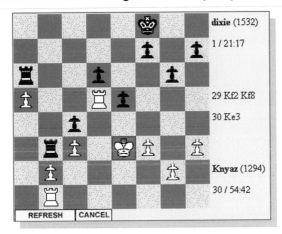

Games software

To play an on-line game, you need a piece of software called a client. This is a program that enables your computer to communicate with the computer on which a particular game program is running. For example, to play a chess game, you will need a chess client.

You can download games clients from the Net. Sometimes you have to pay to use them. Most games pages have hypertext links to the sites where you can download client software.

Logging on

When you are ready to play an on-line game, you need to "log on" to the computer where the game program is running. Log on means you gain access to the computer so that you can use the games program stored on it without transferring it to your own computer. A hypertext link on a games page usually enables you to log on automatically.

MUDs

Multi-User Dungeons, known as MUDs, are popular on-line games. You'll find hundreds of them on the Net. MUD games are adventures that take place in imaginary kingdoms. There are three main types: combat games – where you fight opponents; role play games – in which you play a particular character such as a wizard; and social MUDs - which are based on chatting to other players.

Text or graphics

Most MUDs are text-based. This means that when you meet a monster, you don't see it, you read a description of it. So let your imagination run wild. As you embark on an adventure, text will appear, telling you where you are, what you can see, and giving choices of action. Some MUD games have pictures. They are called graphical or GUI MUDs.

A screen shot from a GUI MUD called Illusia

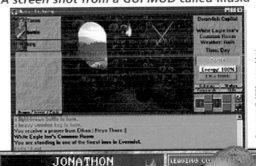

A screen shot from a GUI MUD called Rubies of Eventide and (inset) a goblin from Empires

Problems and solutions

The Internet is sometimes called the Information Superhighway. This description gives many people high expectations of the speed at which information can travel via the Net. Some users are disappointed by problems and congestion which can make the Net slow and frustrating to use. They might call it the Information Dirt-track or the Information Superhypeway.

This section explores some of the problems you may come across on the Net and suggests how to deal with them.

No connection

When you dial up your service provider to go on-line, you may fail to make a connection. The most common cause of this is that too many people are using your ISP's computer and so there are no lines left available. This often happens at times of the day when a lot of people want to use the Net. Redial a few times, but if this doesn't work, try again an hour later.

If you still can't get a connection, telephone your service provider to check that there isn't a fault with their computer.

If you often find that your service provider doesn't have enough telephone lines to deal with all their customers, you might consider finding a service provider with better facilities.

Losing a connection

Once you are on-line, a message may appear telling you that you have lost your connection. This is usually due to your service provider's computer failing. Try connecting again.

Problems on the Net

There are a number of reasons why you may be unable to download Web pages or files successfully. Here are some of them.

 Equipment failure The computers and equipment that make up the Net sometimes break down. All you can do is try again later.

 Wrong address A message, such as Host Not Found, may appear on your screen. This usually means that you have typed in the URL incorrectly. Check carefully that you have used the correct upper and lower case letters and punctuation.

 Change of address You may see a message telling you that the file you require doesn't exist. It may have been removed from the Net, relocated, or had its name changed. Try removing the part of the URL that specifies the exact filename. For example, you might want to look at a photograph with the following address: **http://www.imaginary.co.uk/users/phil_jones/pix/png32.html**. If you typed this in and the file didn't appear, you should try removing the filename, **png32.html**. This might take you to a list of the photographs available and you could resume your search.

 **No access** When trying to use an FTP site, you may be denied access. This is because the computers which store FTP files limit the number of people who are allowed to use them at the same time. This ensures that downloading files doesn't get too slow. Try again later.

 Software problems If you can't get your browser to connect to anything, close it down and reopen it. There may be a mistake in the program, called a bug. This is particularly possible if you are using a beta version of a program (see page 33). If the problem persists, report it to the program's manufacturer.

Congestion

One of the main problems facing the Net is its growing popularity. Every day, more people want to go on-line and do increasingly complicated things, 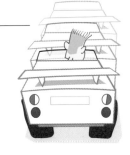 such as downloading video and sound clips. The result is that the Net gets congested with traffic jams of data. This makes everything move more slowly, just like cars on a busy road.

To cope with this problem, new high-speed connections are being built which can handle more data at greater speeds. But these improvements take time and money.

In the meantime, it's a good idea to avoid the busiest times on the Net, which tend to be when people in the USA are using it. This is because most of the resources on the Net are based in the USA.

 How many?

People have calculated that if the number of Net users continues growing at its current rate, everyone in the world will be on-line by the year 2001. This is nonsense, of course, because in many countries people can't afford to buy computers.

Cutting costs

Going on-line doesn't have to be expensive. You don't need to buy a high-speed modem, a super-fast computer or expensive software. Here are some ways in which you can enjoy all the Net has to offer without spending a fortune.
• If your computer isn't powerful, which means that it can't process data quickly, don't use a Web browser, like Netscape Navigator, that can access newsgroups and send e-mail as well as browse the Web. Programs like this are complicated, and will make your computer run slowly. Choose individual programs to use newsgroups, e-mails and FTP. These programs are older and simpler, and will use less of your computer's memory.
• If you don't have a high speed modem, make sure that you minimize the amount of data you need to download.

One way of doing this is to instruct your browser to download only the text of Web pages, not the pictures. You can find out how to do this on page 20.
• Remember that all the programs you will need are available free on the Net.  You can find out the URL addresses of where to go to download some useful programs on page 42.
• If you are charged for the amount of time you are on line, always write e-mails and newsgroup articles before you are connected up.
• Avoid using the Net at times of the day when telephone calls are charged at an expensive rate.
• If you only want to use the Net for e-mail or newsgroups, you can use a local company, called a Bulletin Board Service (BBS), or a service provider, to provide you with access to these facilities. This costs less than a full Internet access connection.

Safety Net

With millions of people using the Net, there are bound to be those who misuse it. Here are some useful guidelines that will ensure the Net is a safe place for you to surf.

 Don't give your e-mail address to strangers. You don't want to receive lots of unwanted e-mail. Just think, you wouldn't give your snail mail address to a complete stranger, would you?

 Someone you chat to on the Net may suggest meeting up in real life (known as "boinking"). If you want to go, make sure you arrange to meet in a public place, where you will feel safe.

 You should always be aware that it is easy for people to play pranks or pretend to be something they aren't on the Net. For instance, you might meet an adult pretending to be a child.

 When you send information via the Net, it passes from one computer to another until it reaches its destination. If somebody gained access to a Net computer, they could use your information dishonestly. Don't send personal details, such as your home address, phone number, or financial details, such as a credit card number, via the Net.

There are some Web sites where financial details are safe. The information is coded so that it can't be used by anyone else.

 People are free to publish whatever they like on the Net. So, as well as interesting things, there's also unpleasant, unsuitable and dangerous information out there. Be careful to avoid anything you don't want to look at.

There are programs available that will check the information you download from the Net for offensive words, and block access to certain Web sites.

 Computer viruses are programs which can damage the data stored on your computer. Every day new viruses are being invented by people who want to harm the Net.

Your computer can catch a virus over the Net if you copy files from an infected computer. Make sure that you have anti-virus software installed on your computer. This will check your hard disk for certain viruses. Update this software regularly to catch new viruses.

 Hackers are people who access computer systems without permission. They can link up their own computers to networks, and open private files. By changing the information in these files, they may be able to steal money or goods.

If you have private information stored on your computer, make sure you set up your system to prevent people connecting to it. If you are using a computer at home, it is unlikely that people can access your files.

Net potatoes

Some people predict that by the year 2000, people will spend more time surfing the Net than they spend watching television.

Some Net facilities, such as games and IRC, can become very addictive. Remember, using a computer for any purpose for long periods of time can damage your health.

It's essential to take a ten minute break every hour that you use a computer. This will rest your eyes and other parts of your body.

There's more to life than surfing the Net. So make sure you don't become a Net potato and end up at the receiving end of a common Net insult... GAL, which means Get A Life!

Providing a service

Here are the e-mail addresses and telephone numbers of companies who can get you on-line. For a wider selection, look in Internet magazines and local newspapers.

Service providers

Over 2000 companies world-wide offer access to the Net.

North America
Delphi Internet Services Corp.
service@delphi.com
1 800 695 4005

Pipeline
info@pipeline.com
1 800 453 7473

Netcom
info@netcom.com
1 800 353 6600

PSINet Inc.
info@psi.com
1 800 827 7482

SprintLink
info@sprintlink.net
1 800 817 7755

WinNET Communications Inc.
info@win.net
1 502 589 6800

Great Britain
BT Internet
support@btinternet.com
0345 776666

Demon Internet Ltd
sales@demon.net
0181 371 1234

Easynet Ltd
info@easynet.co.uk
0171 209 0990

PSINet UK Ltd
sales@uk.psi.com
01223 577577

UUNet Pipex Ltd
sales@dial.pipex.com
0500 474739

RedNet Ltd
info@red.net
01494 513333

Ireland
Ireland On-Line
sales@iol.ie
01 855 1739

Europe
Individual Network e.V. (Germany)
in-info@individual.net
0441 9808556

Netland (Netherlands)
info@netland.nl
020 6943664

FranceNet (France)
infos@FranceNet.fr
1 43 92 14 49

Australia
Ausnet Services Pty Ltd
sales@world.net
1 800 806 755

OzEmail Pty Ltd
sales@ozemail.com.au
1 800 805 874

Hong Kong
Hong Kong Supernet
info@hk.super.net
2358 7924

WorldLink Communication Ltd
info@wlink.net
2111 3333

New Zealand
Internet Company of NZ
help@icons.co.nz
09 358 1186

South Africa
UUnet Internet Africa
webmaster@iafrica.com
0800 020 003

On-line services

CompuServe
1 800 848 8990 (US)
0800 289 378 (UK)
0990 412 412 (International)

America Online
1 800 827 6364 (US)
0800 279 1234 (UK)

IBM Global Network
0800 973 000 (Europe, Asia, Middle East)
1 800 821 4612 (USA)

Microsoft Network
Follow the instructions on your Windows 95 program.

Searching on-line

If you can go on-line for a trial session, you'll find a list of service providers at the news-group: **alt.internet.services** or look at the Web site:
http://www.best.be/iap/
    Alternatively, you could go to:
http://www.yahoo.com/.
In the menus that appear click on the following: Computers and Internet → Internet → Commercial Services → Internet Access Providers → Regional → Countries
Then select the country you wish to view.

Sites and resources

Here is a selection of the useful and fun things you can find on the Net. Type the URLs into your browser exactly as they are shown here.

Sites for Internet software

The following sites have information and links to a variety of Internet software.
Windows 95
http://www.windows95.com/

Windows
http://cws.internet.com/

Mac
**http://wwwhost.ots.utexas.edu/mac/
internet.html**

OS/2
http://www.teamos2.org/

Amiga
http://www.germany.aminet.org/aminet

Netscape home page, with links to browser software
http://home.netscape.com/

Programs for compressing and inflating files
PKZip
http://www.pkware.com/
WinZip for Windows
http://www.winzip.com/
Stuffit for Macs
http://www.aladdinsys.com/index.html

Web Phone, an Internet telephone
http://www.netspeak.com/

CU-SeeMe, video conferencing home page
http://cu-seeme.cornell.edu/

IRC client software
(for Windows) **http://www.mirc.co.uk/**
(for Macs) **http://www.xs4all.nl/~ircle/**

MUD client software information
http://www.avalon.co.uk/clientsw.html

Graphical and VR MUD client software
http://www.chaco.com/pueblo/

Hot sites for kids

The following are great sites for kids to visit.
The Exploratorium, a science and technology museum
http://www.exploratorium.edu/

Kidlink, on-line chat for kids
http://www.kidlink.org/IRC/

Fishnet, a magazine for teenagers
http://www.jayi.com/jayi/

Lists of interesting sites for children
http://db.cochran.com/li_toc:theopage.db
http://www.ability.org.uk/children.html

Disney's home page
http://www.disney.com/

Whoopie, an index of sound and video clips
http://www.whoopie.com/

Games

A selection of sites for information about games and links to games software.
Caissa home page, on-line chess
http://caissa.com/info.html

Games Domain, all kinds of games information
http://www.gamesdomain.co.uk/

Nintendo's home page
http://www.nintendo.com/

Sega's home page
http://www.sega.com/

GameSpot, videogames links and support
http://www.gamespot.com/

The MUDlist, MUD links and information
http://mudlist.kharduin.net/

Graphical MUDs, lists and links
**http://www.mudconnector.com/
mud_graphical.html**

Links to Worlds Chat and AlphaWorld VR games
http://www.worlds.net/

A glossary of Internet words

Here's a list of some of the Internet words you may come across and their meanings. The definitions are specific to the use of the words in relation to the Net. Some words have other meanings in different contexts.

Any word that appears in *italic* type is defined elsewhere in the glossary.

acronym   Words that are usually made up of the first letters of a phrase or saying, such as BFN, which is an acronym for Bye For Now.

address   A description of where to find a piece of information on the Net.

anonymous FTP   To transfer files across the Net you need to use *FTP*. Anonymous FTP is when you can transfer them without using a special user code or password.

applet   A small program written in a programming language called *Java*. The applet might be inserted into a *Web page*.

application   A program that allows you to do something useful with your computer.

Archie   A program that helps locate *FTP* files anywhere on the Internet.

archive   A file or files that have been grouped together. They may have been compressed so that they are smaller.

article   A message sent to a *newsgroup* or a *mailing list*.

attachment   A file, such as a picture file, sent with an *e-mail* message.

avatar   A small on-screen picture which represents the body of a player in a *Virtual Reality* game.

backbone   A link between computers that carries a lot of information very quickly and usually over a long distance.

bandwidth   The capacity of a link between computers to transfer data, measured in *bits* per second (*bps*).

beta   A newly written program that is made available to be tested by users.

BBS   (Bulletin Board System). A system that allows people to leave messages and read messages left by other people.

bit   The smallest unit of computer data.

body   The part of an *e-mail* in which the message appears.

bps   (bits per second). The unit used to measure how fast information is transmitted by a *modem*.

browser   A program used to find and look at documents stored on the Net.

chat   Conversations held with other users via the Net.

client   A program that enables a computer to use the services provided by other computers.

connect time   The length of time spent connected to the Net.

country code   The part of the name for an Internet computer that indicates what country it is in.

crash   A sudden failure in a computer system.

Cybercafés   Cafés at which people can use computers to access the Net.

dialer   A program that instructs a *modem* to telephone another computer.

dial up   Use telephone lines to connect one computer to another to go *on-line*.

DNS   (Domain Name System). A system of giving computers on the Net names that are easy for users to remember.

domain   Part of the name for an Internet computer that specifies its location and whether it is in a commercial, educational or government organization.

down   The word used to describe computer equipment that is not working.

download   To copy files from another computer onto your own computer.

e-mail   (electronic mail). A way of sending messages via computers.

emoticon *see* **smiley**

encryption   Using a secret code so that people cannot read files without permission.

FAQ   (Frequently Asked Questions). A document used by *newsgroups* which lists the answers to the questions commonly asked by new members.

follow up   An *article* sent to a *newsgroup* commenting on a previously posted article.

freeware   *Software* that is free to use.
FTP   (File Transfer Protocol). The system used to transfer files from one computer to another over the Net.

Gopher   A program which searches the Net for information by picking options from menus.
GUI   (Graphical User Interface). A system that uses on-screen pictures which can be clicked on with a mouse to give a computer instructions.

hacker   Someone who gains unauthorized access to a computer to look at, change or destroy data.
hardware   The equipment that makes up a computer *network*.
header   The information at the start of a document that tells a computer what to do with it. An *e-mail* header, for example, contains information about the address of the recipient and the sender.
helper application   A program which enables a *browser* to perform extra tasks, such as playing sound clips.
hit   When someone looks at a *Web site*. The number of hits a particular page receives is counted to see how popular it is.
home page   An introductory page containing links to other pages on a *Web site*. The page that a *browser* displays when you start using it, is also called the home page.
host   A computer connected to the Net.
HTML   (HyperText Mark-up Language). The language used to create documents on the *World Wide Web*.
HTTP   (HyperText Transfer Protocol). The system used to transfer *hypertext* documents over the Net.
hypertext   A document that contains high-lighted text or pictures linked to other documents. When you click on hypertext, the linked document will be *downloaded*.

icon   A picture you can click on to make your computer do something, or which appears to indicate that your computer is doing something.
Internet (or the Net)   A computer *network* made up of millions of linked computers.

Internet service providers (ISPs) also known as
Internet access providers (IAPs)   Companies that sell Net connections to people.
IP   (Internet Protocol). The system used to specify how data is transferred over the Net.
IP address   The unique number given to each computer on the Net.
IRC   (Internet Relay Chat). A way of having a conversation with other Net users by typing messages and reading their responses.
ISDN   (Integrated Services Digital Network). A type of high speed telephone line which can transmit data between computers very quickly.
java   A language used to write programs which enables *Web pages* to include interesting features such as animations.

link   1. A connection between two computers. 2. The highlighted text or pictures in a *hypertext* document.
log   A file which keeps a record of the files you have used and changed, things that have happened and messages received during an *on-line* session.
log on/log in   Connect a computer to another computer.

mailbox   The place where *e-mail* is kept for a user by an *Internet service provider*.
mailing list   A discussion group where articles are posted to the members of the group using *e-mail*.
mail server   A computer that handles *e-mail*.
menu   A list of options from which a user selects.
MIME   (Multipurpose Internet Mail Extensions). A way of sending files attached to *e-mail*.
modem   (MOdulate/DEModulate). A device that allows computer data to be sent down a telephone line.
moderated   A *newsgroup* or *mailing list* in which articles sent in are not immediately sent out to all the users. First they go to a person, who decides whether they are suitable.
MUD   (Multi-User Dungeon). A game which lots of people can play at the same time, if they are all connected, via the Net, to a computer that is running the game.

network A number of computers and other devices that are linked together so that they can share information and equipment.

network computer A special computer designed exclusively to be used on a *network* such as the Net.

newsgroup A place where people with the same interests can *post* messages and see other people's responses.

newsreader A program that lets you send and read the messages in *newsgroups*.

node Any computer attached to the Net.

off-line Not connected to the Net.

on-line Connected to the Net.

on-line service A company that gives you access to its private *network*, containing various kinds of information, and usually gives you access to the Net.

packet A chunk of information sent over the Net.

page A document or chunk of information available on the *Web*.

plug-in A program you can add to your *browser* that enables it to perform extra functions, such as displaying video clips or 3-D images.

POP (Point Of Presence) A point of access to the Net, usually a computer owned by an *Internet service provider*.

post Placing a message in a *newsgroup* so that other members can read it.

protocol A set of rules that two computers agree to use when communicating with each other.

serial port The part of a computer through which data can be transmitted. *Modems* are connected to computers through serial ports.

server A computer or the *software* on a computer, that makes itself available for other computers to use.

set-top box A special piece of computer equipment that connects to your TV and lets you access the Net using the TV as a screen.

shareware *Software* which you can try out before you have to pay for it.

signature file A file, often a picture or a quotation, attached to the end of an *e-mail*.

site 1. A collection of *Web pages* set up by an organization or individual. 2. A computer *network* that is joined to the Net.

smiley A picture, made up from characters on the keyboard, which looks like a face and is used to add emotion to a typed message.

software Programs that enable computers to carry out certain tasks.

subscribe Add your address to a *mailing list* or *newsgroup*.

TCP/IP The language which computers on the Net use to communicate with each other.

Telnet A program that allows you to connect your computer to another computer so that you can interact with it. This might mean using its database, or playing a multiplayer game (see *MUD*).

thread A sequence of articles sent to a *newsgroup* forming a discussion on a particular subject.

timeout When a computer gives up attempting to carry out a particular function, because it has taken too long.

up A word used to describe a computer that is functioning.

upload To copy programs from your computer onto another computer on the Net.

URL (Uniform or Universal Resource Locator). The system by which all the different resources on the Net are given an address.

Usenet A collection of *newsgroups*.

Virtual Reality (VR) The use of 3-D computer pictures (called graphics) to create an imaginary world which surrounds a user.

virus A program specially designed to interfere with other programs and files.

World Wide Web (also known as **WWW** or the **Web**) Part of the Net made up of pages of information linked together by *hypertext* links.

zip A program used to compress files to make them smaller.

Net slang

Lots of slang words are used in connection with the Internet. Here are some of the most common ones.

All the words that appear in *italic* type are defined in the glossary on pages 43 to 45.

boinking Meeting face to face someone with whom you have made contact on the Net.

bounce When *e-mail* fails to get through to its destination.

box A computer.

braindump Saying everything you know about a topic, but more than your audience really wants to hear.

clickstream The path you take around the Net by clicking on *hypertext* links.

Cyberspace The imaginary space that you travel around in when you use the Net.

dead tree edition The paper version of a book or article that is also available on the *Net*.

electronic anarchy The state of freedom and lawlessness that exists on the Net. There are few rules and restrictions, so you can do and say what you want.

electrotransvestism Pretending to be a member of the opposite sex when sending messages over the Net.

eyeball search To read a page on-screen.

eye candy Programs which look nice, but aren't particularly useful.

flame bait A controversial *newsgroup* message that is likely to attract angry messages.

flame mail Angry or rude messages sent to a member or members of a *newsgroup*.

flame war An argument carried out by members of a *newsgroup*.

gronk out What you do when you have had enough of using the Net and stop for the day.

Infobahn, Information Superhighway
Slang words for the Internet.

lurking Reading the messages sent to a *newsgroup* without sending any yourself.

Net cop, **Net judge** or **Net police** Someone who thinks it is their duty to tell other Net users how to behave. These terms are usually insults.

Net evangelist Someone who tries to persuade other people to start using the Net.

Net guru An expert who is respected for their knowledge of the Net and how it works.

Netiquette Rules about the proper way to behave when using the Net.

Net surfer Someone who travels around the Net looking for interesting places to visit and people to talk to.

Net surfing or surfing on the Net Exploring the Net by jumping from one file to another, like a surfer catching one wave and then another.

Net traffic Data moving around on the Net.

Net users - Netters, Netsters, Netizens Netheads, Netoisie, Internauts,

Infonauts Names for people who use the Net.

newbie A new Net user or a new member of a *newsgroup*.

newbie hunting Looking out for new Net users who aren't sure of what they are doing, and teasing them.

noise An ongoing conversation in a *newsgroup*. Noise usually implies that it is a conversation which isn't very relevant to the topic of the *newsgroup*.

shouting Writing messages in UPPER CASE letters lets everyone know that you are angry.

snail mail Normal mail delivered by the post office, as opposed to *e-mail* sent over the Net.

spamming Sending lots of messages to a *newsgroup*, a *mailing list* or an individual.

virtual journey The imaginary distances you travel to sites on the Net, even though you stay in one place.

virtual relationship A friendship or relationship that starts on the Net.

wired Feeling odd from having spent too much time staring at a computer screen. It can also simply mean connected to the Net.

Index

Acknowledgements

Screen shots

Every effort has been made to trace the copyright holders of the material in this book. If any rights have been omitted, the publishers offer their sincere apologies and will rectify this in any subsequent editions following notification.

The material on Web sites changes from time to time. Usborne Publishing Ltd cannot be held responsible for the suitability of anything that may appear on the sites listed below.

Screen shots used with permission from Microsoft Corporation. Microsoft and Microsoft Windows are registered trademarks of Microsoft Corporation in the US and other countries.

p.3   Netscape. Copyright © The Netscape Communications logo is a trademark of Netscape Communications Corporation.
http://home.netscape.com/
p.6/7   Rusti Sprokit. All rights copyright © 1996 crisp wreck. Unauthorized reproduction and/or sale is prohibited and subject to intergalactic criminal prosecution. Used by permission. WebPhone is a trademark of NetSpeak Corporation. Patents pending.
http://www.netspeak.com/
RadioNet. Copyright © 1996 T.P.I. GmbH - the mediaw@re company - designed by Klaus Eisermann
http://www.radio-net.com/hpengl.htm
Visible Human Project
http://www.hlm.nih.gov/
The White House for Kids
http://www1.whitehouse.gov/WH/kids/html/kidshome.html
The Art of China
http://pasture.ecn.purdue.edu/~agenhtml/agenmc/china/china.html
CU-SeeMe. Copyright © 1993, 1994, 1995, Cornell University
http://cu-seeme.cornell.edu/
AlphaWorld. Copyright © 1995-1996 Worlds Inc.
http://worlds.net/alphaworld/
The original unofficial Elvis home page
http://sunsite.unc.edu/elvis/elvishom.html
Cyberkids. Copyright © 1995-96 Mountain Lake Software, Inc. Used with permission.
http://www.cyberkids.com/
Eurostar. Used with permission.
http://www.eurostar.com/eurostar/
World Bank. Copyright © The International Bank for Reconstruction and Development/The World Bank
http://www.worldbank.org/
Europe Online weather map. Copyright © 1996 Europe Online S.A
p.9   Computer Network connections on the NSFNET © NCSA, University of Illinois/Science Photo Library
Cyberia Paris. Copyright © Frederick Froument
p.12   CompuServe   **http://www.compuserve.com/**
Demon   **http://www.demon.net/**
Pipex   **http://www.uunet.pipex.com/**
Individual Network e.V.   **http://www.north.de/ings/**
America Online   **http://www.aol.com/**
p.14   Pipex Dial screen shots © Pipex Dial is a registered trade mark of the Public Exchange Ltd trading as UUNET Pipex. All rights reserved.
P.16/17   With thanks to Nasa
http://www.nasa.gov/
p.18   AltaVista. Copyright © 1996 Digital Equipment Corporation. All rights reserved.
http://altavista.digital.com/

p.19   YAHOOLIGANS! and the YAHOOLIGANS! logo are trademarks of YAHOO!, Inc. Text and artwork copyright © 1996 by YAHOO!, Inc. All rights reserved.
http://www.yahooligans.com/
With thanks to Alaska State Museums
http://ccl.alaska.edu/local/museum/home.html
p.20   Cyberkids. Copyright © 1995-96 Mountain Lake Software, Inc. Used with permission.
http://www.cyberkids.com/
p.21   Copyright © When Saturday Comes, 1996
http://www.dircon.co.uk/wsc/
Cosmix Solar System, Philip Hallstrom / philiph@cosmix.com. Copyright 1996, Cosmix Web Design
http://www.cosmix.com/playground/java/planets/
p.34   WebPhone is a trademark of NetSpeak Corporation. Patents pending.
http://www.netspeak.com/
CU-SeeMe. Copyright © 1993, 1994, 1995, Cornell University
http://cu-seeme.cornell.edu
p.35   Alpha World and Worlds Chat screenshots. Copyright © 1995-1996 Worlds Inc.
http://www.worlds.net/
p.36   Nintendo. Copyright © Nintendo of America, 1996
http://www.nintendo.com/
Sega. Copyright © 1995 SEGA, P.O. Box 8097 Redwood City, CA 94065. All Rights Reserved.
http://www.sega.com/
Sailor Moon Support Site. Copyright © 1996 Sailor Moon Support Site.
http://www.hkstar.com/~chimo/
Grand Prix II. Copyright © Microprose Ltd.
http://www.microprose.com/gamesdesign/gp2/
p.37   Caissa Online Chess. Copyright © 1995-1996 Mediawest Online. Caissa's Web is a trademark of Mediawest Online.
http://caissa.com/info.html
Illusia. Copyright © 1995 Living Mask Productions
http://www.illusia.com/illusia.html
Empires. Copyright © 1996 Dan Bradley
http://ucsu.colorado.edu/~woehr/
Rubies of Eventide. Copyright © 1996 by Cyber Warrior, Inc. All rights reserved.
http://www.cyberwar.com/rubies.html

Computer equipment

p.10/11   Online Media set-top box produced by Acorn Computer Group plc.
Gateway 2000 computer used by permission of Gateway. ACCURA™ 288 Message Modem and the OPTIMA™ V.34 + FAX PC Card were supplied by Hayes Microcomputer Products, Inc., the inventor of the PC modem.

ISBN 0-590-63160-8

12 11 10 9 8 7 6 5 4 3 2   8 9/9 0 1 2 3/0

Printed in the U.S.A.   24

First Scholastic printing, September 1998